The book of Isaiah is the longest prophetic book of the Jewish Bible. He prophesied during the reign of king Ahaz, of Judah. Isaiah's book contains so many prophecies regarding the Messiah and His kingdom. Isaiah is often called, the Messianic prophet. On a sad note, Isaiah was martyred during the reign of Manasseh. According to history, he apparently was sawed in half.

A quote from this Messianic prophet is a fitting tribute to start this book. A special thanks to Lori Elder for her help in suggesting this verse from the Bible.

> "And an highway shall be there, and a way, and it shall be called The way of holiness; the unclean shall not pass over it; but it shall be for those: the wayfaring men, though fools, shall not err therein." - Isaiah 35:8

SALVATION HIGHWAY

Have you ever wondered, "Where is God?" Do you acknowledge a savior? Is prayer part of your daily routine like eating and washing? This book delves into many topics regarding mankind's relationship with God.

For my loyal readers, be sure to write to me at my e-mail address, jimhewittwriting@aol.com. When I receive your e-mail, I will add you to my SPECIAL e-mail list. This group of readers will receive updates on any already published subject matter. In addition, any time I publish a new book they will know about it in advance.

Titles written by James Hewitt

Sick Building Syndrome
The Christmas Tree
Memory: Lost & Found
The Adirondack Cookbook
Word Soup

Salvation Highway

James Hewitt, RN

No part of this publication may be reproduced, stored in a retrieval system, or transmitted in any form or by any means, electronic, mechanical, photocopying, recording, or otherwise, without written permission of the publisher.

ISBN: 978-0-578-02725-8

GNU Free Documentation License

Copyright 2009 by James P. Hewitt

Published by Lulu Distribution (www.lulu.com)

Printed with pride in the USA.

"We may not pay Satan reverence, for that would be indiscreet, but we can at least respect his talents."
- Mark Twain

"Nobody shoots at Santa Claus."
- Alfred Emanuel Smith

"Vengeance is mine; I will repay, says the Lord."
- Romans 12:19

"Then the eyes of the blind shall be opened, and the ears of the deaf shall be unstopped." - Isaiah 35:5

"While the earth remaineth, seedtime and harvest, and cold and heat, and summer and winter, and day and night shall not cease." - Genesis 8:22

GOD 12

Thanks

Thanks to all who gave me their valuable input.

A special thanks to Bishop Daniel Elder and his wife Lori for their many readings and corrections of any religious based errors. They are a true font of biblical information. The Peru Word of God parish is lucky to have such a great asset.

Bill Rutz, is a friend, co-worker, and fellow Christian. Bill, thanks for all your help with the Scriptures and motivational talks. You and your family hold a special place in my heart.

Table of Contents

Dedication
Power of a Dream
Introduction
Where is God?
Separation of Church and State
Pledge of Allegiance and Timeline
In God We Trust and Timeline
Ten Commandments
School Prayer
Faith Based Initiatives
Evolution Versus Genesis
Are We Better With or Without God?
Church Etiquette
Breakdown of Worldwide Religions
Conclusion
Religious Web Sites
Glossary
References
About the Author

"Be just and fear not"

Dedication

This book is dedicated to all of the men and women who have dedicated their life's work to spreading the word of God. This book is dedicated to you and the good work you do. Humanity appreciates the long hours, the sacrifices, and the dedication you have for your vocation.

This book also honors religious martyrs. A religious martyr is a person who voluntarily suffers death rather than denies his or her religion. They gave the ultimate sacrifice to show their love for God, by giving their life.

All of the money earned from the sale of this book will be given to support Missionary works throughout the world. This money will help to honor these dedicated people and the martyr's.

> "I know thy works, and where thou dwellest, even where Satan's seat is: and thou holdest fast my name, and hast not denied my faith, even in those days wherein Antipas was my faithful martyr, who was slain among you, where Satan dwelleth." - Rev 2:13

Mother Teresa

Power of a Dream

This book was created, due to a dream. One night I had a dream that I was sitting on a dock fishing. An older gentleman, who looked a little like Ernest Hemingway sat down next to me to talk. He told me how in his day they fished with nets. I told him that I did not think nets were legal in the United States. He replied, "Back then the United States wasn't around". I asked him his name. He told me that I already knew his name. I politely told him that I had never seen him before. He said back in his youth he was called, Yahweh.

> "He hath said, which heard the words of God, which saw the vision of the Almighty, falling into a trance, but having his eyes open:" - Num 24:4

He told me that everyone has a special gift. My special God given gift is the ability to put word to paper. Yahweh told me that mankind has been pushing him away for the last few centuries, but when something bad happens, they pray to him and ask him, "Why did it happen?".

In my dream, I was freaking out. I asked him what he wanted with me. God told me that he has only one mission for him. He informed me that he is sad. Why, was my reply? He said, "I created man and love him like my son. I love man so much that I took on man's form, as Jesus. Man has been gradually pushing me away. As a parent figure, I know that every child must venture out on their own, but they should always keep their parents close to heart. Man has forgotten this."

Once again, I asked him what he wanted with me. He asked me that same question in reverse. My reply was, "to have a healthy family and loving children". He sighed and said that our desires were of a similar nature, for every parent in their heart loves their children. At this point, he looked me square in the eye and said that my only mission is to spread the word. I asked stupidly what word. He laughed and said, "The Word of God". His laugh was amazing. It was a cross between a Santa laugh and the infectious laughter of a child. I asked, "How can I spread the word". He said, "Spread my word through paper". At this point, he stood up as to leave. I told him I would try and he said, "I love you, like your Father, John loves you. Spread the word". At those words, he started to dissipate and was gone.

At this point, I woke up drenched in a sweat. I quickly did an internet search for Yahweh and found that it is the Aramaic name for "God". Who am I to argue. It is up to you to determine whether you believe. This book is the proof of my belief.

> "I saw a dream which made me afraid, and the thoughts upon my bed and the visions of my head troubled me." - Dan 4:5

Introduction

Do you know Jesus? That is the question all Christians will ask when attempting to engage an non-believer in conversation. Referring to Jesus Christ on a first name basis indicates a certain level of friendship. We refer to friends, close co-workers, and family on a first name basis. Other people we address them by their surname or last name. Yet is that true for the average believer in modern Christianity? None of us has physically met Jesus. Should we refer to him as Mr. Christ? Jesus' love for mankind is what breaks through this social custom. Knowing Jesus makes a follower feel like a close friend. It also makes us feel like a part of his family. Makes you wonder though, "How well does the Christian today know Jesus?"

We live in a society that is increasingly hostile to Christians and people of every faith. America has become a nation where public school students are prohibited from praying in school, acknowledging their dependence upon God, and forming religious clubs. American society has openly challenged its schools and communities from displaying nativity scenes, the Ten Commandments, and other symbols of our religious and moral heritage. Our country was founded on the principles of freedom. It is a sad state of affairs when the only time people acknowledge God's existence is when they face a hardship, a trying time or a loss, and desire his help.

How many times in our life have we asked ourselves, "Where is God?" or "Why did God let this happen?" Most of us have at one time pondered this question, especially when facing a hardship. Unfortunately, there is no simple answer that will satisfy everyone. The answer has more to do with His presence in our lives than with our belief in His existence. We want to know, where is God when it hurts? Where is God when something goes desperately wrong in my life? As a Registered Nurse, I often wonder why God lets people suffer and children perish, especially since he has the power to prevent all this suffering and loss of life.

Our Lord and Savior Jesus Christ Was Born

"Look upon mine affliction and my pain; and forgive all my sins." - Psalm 25:18

Our conclusions depend on what we rely on as a benchmark for truth in our lives. Do you believe the Bible is true, and that it is what it claims to be? If you do, then you recognize that it is the very Word of God. The Bible is a great place to begin looking for His presence. The Bible contains many of the answers to your questions and problems. Have you ever read the entire Bible, both Old and New Testaments? When was the last time you started or ended the day reading the Bible? Try it and you may find that it makes a difference in your life.

In this book, I plan to discuss some of the major challenges organized religions face. I will discuss Where is God, the Separation of Church and State, Pledge of Allegiance, In God We Trust, the Ten Commandments, School Prayer, George Bush's Faith Based Initiative, Evolution versus Genesis, Are We Better With or Without God, and give a breakdown of worldwide religions. I also have included the most common religions web sites and a glossary of terms.

This book is not broken into chapters, but sections. Read the sections that interest you, but I hope that you will read them all. Every Christian possesses a spiritual gift. The biblical perspective of the spiritual gift, projects that God in His sovereign will has bestowed the ability upon each believer to administrate ministry to others in the power of the Holy Spirit. This enables believers to exemplify the Lord Jesus Christ. Spiritual Gifts are presented in scripture as a means of provoking good works and spiritual soundness within the Body of Christ for the glory of God. The gift of knowledge is essential to ministering to others.

Where is God?

Where is God? In today's fast and modern world, it is very easy for us to think that we suffer alone. Remember that as you have wondered where is God, so has someone else. My Dad always said, "In life there is always someone worse off than you." I believe that God allows suffering to teach us something. How would we learn anything if there wasn't suffering or trials that we have to go through? To keep our faith we need to be tested. Trials and tribulations are a form of testing. If you can get through the hard times and still Praise God, then you have accomplished a great deal.

Here is another way to look at life's lessons from God. When you are a child and you do something wrong, your parents correct you. Whether it is by a spanking or by a time out, it is still a form of punishment or suffering for what you did wrong. You mess up, you pay the consequences, and you learn from your mistakes. If you don't make mistakes and aren't punished, then how will you learn anything at all. God is in a way our supreme parent. We are all children of God.

Alexander Solzhenitsyn said, "The entire 20th century is being sucked into the vortex of atheism and self-destruction. We can only reach with determination for the warm hand of God, which we have so rashly and self-confidently pushed away. There is nothing else to cling to in the landslide."

I have realized through all my readings of the

descriptions and viewpoints of many different religions, that it appears the intent of any religion is to better ourselves, give us answers, and most importantly, help us find peace. If that really is the case, then I ask you, can believing in a god do us any harm? If people had more faith and respect for God, I believe that society would have fewer problems. Simply put, if everyone had a smidgen of faith, the world would be a better place.

Most of the world's religions do not fully understand it, but the real antidote to the fear caused by sudden catastrophes, or even by problems in our personal lives, is to have a real, "living" faith. Health problems, marital problems, financial worries, and fears concerning the future can all be alleviated, understood, and even solutions can be arrived at, through faith and by having a relationship with God.

Religion is usually programmed in us by our parents before we truly understand it. Whether you're Christian, Jewish, Muslim, Buddhist, Agnostic, Atheist, or otherwise, your religious outlook on life has an influence in everything you do. The choice to believe or not believe in God often dictates your stance on many of life's big issues like abortion, the death penalty, gun control, and even education.

What is faith? Do you have it? How do you know? Can you see, touch, smell, or hear it? To many people, faith is a warm and positive feeling. It may be a promise they think comes from a God they do not really know, but is in some way watching over them. Do you go to your church looking for answer? Do you eventually go home having learned nothing of value, disappointed because there weren't any answers?

Faith, in my opinion is best summed up by a verse from The English Version of the Bible, "To have faith is to be sure of the things we hope for, to be certain of the things we cannot see."

As we all grow as Christian's in our relationship with God, we will find ourselves increasingly compelled to serve others in the likeness of Jesus Christ for the greater glory of God. As Christians, we are instructed to use our spiritual gifts for the benefit of Christ. The key to knowing and applying our spiritual gift is through a sound study of God's Word, which is the Bible and through communication with God in the form of prayer.

To follow God and be a faithful Christian, a follower must be willing to adhere to God's standard of worship. This standard is found in John 4:23 where true followers are described as worshiping God "in spirit and in truth." To worship God in truth means that each of us must be willing to see things from

God's point of view. As impossible as it may be, we must put ourselves in God's shoes. We must see and interpret things for what they truly are, and not from what we have been conditioned to believe.

> "Knowing what to say makes for an effective ministry." - 1 Cor. 12:8

Separation of Church and State

      The United States of America was founded upon the ideals of religious freedom. When the Pilgrims sailed to America to live and set up the first colonies back in 1620, it was to escape religious persecution. The Pilgrims dreamed of a nation where they could have their own beliefs and be free from their tyrannical King. Early immigrants to the American colonies came, because they were motivated largely by the desire to worship freely in their own fashion.

"Restore unto me the joy of thy salvation; and uphold me with thy free spirit." - Psl 51:12

      The rulers of many ancient cultures claimed that they were given their powers through the divine right of a supreme being. Divine right is the belief that the power to rule is bestowed upon the ruler by a supreme being. This gave the rulers the power to govern all the lands of their country, as well in many cases to be the head of that religion. First came God and then the ruler came second only to God. The ruler was chosen by God to be the ruler and speaker for God.

      The definition of Divine Right from dictionary.com sums it all up perfectly. "Divine right is the doctrine that kings derive their right to rule directly from God and are not accountable to their subjects." The idea of rule through the divine right doctrine was based on the idea that rulers derived their right to rule by virtue of their birth alone. This is a right based on the law of God and of nature.

Authority is transmitted to the current ruler from his ancestors, whom God himself appointed to rule. The sovereign was responsible and answerable not to the governed, but to God alone, so any active resistance to a king was deemed a sin against God and thus ensuring damnation. It is tough to stand up for your beliefs when the alternative is going to hell.

When the United States of America was founded, it represented the most progressive movement in Western Civilization since the days of the Greek democracies. The movement for revolution, was sparked by Thomas Paine, who roused the colonists' desire for freedom.

The first idea in the new colonies regarding the idea of religion being separated from government occurred in December 27 1657, with the Flushing Remonstrance. The Flushing Remonstrance was the forerunner to the first amendment of the U.S. Constitution. The first amendment gives people the freedom of religion, speech, press, assembly, and to petition the Government for a redress of grievances.

The Flushing Remonstrance petition was signed by a group of thirty English citizens in America who were being persecuted by the Quakers, due to the religious policies set in place by the Governor of New Netherland, Peter Stuyvesant. The citizens who signed the petition were not Quakers. This petition requested an exemption to Stuyvesant's ban on Quaker worship. Flushing is located in present day Queens, New York. Back then, it was part of the Dutch colony of the New Netherland.

Quaker

According to Free Dictionary.com, the definition of the US Constitution is, "a document embodying the fundamental principles upon which the American republic is conducted." Listed below are the two Amendments that pertain to religious rights.

Amendment One states, "Congress shall make no law respecting an establishment of religion, or prohibiting the free exercise thereof; or abridging the freedom of speech, or of the press; or the right of the people peaceably to assemble, and to petition the Government for a redress of grievances."

Amendment Fourteen, Article One states, "All persons born or naturalized in the United States, and subject to the jurisdiction thereof, are citizens of the United States and of the State wherein they reside. No State shall make or enforce any law which shall abridge the privileges or immunities of citizens of the United States; nor shall any State deprive any person of life, liberty, or property, without due process of law; nor deny to any person within its jurisdiction the equal protection of the laws." This amendment was the provision that provided slaves equal rights under the Constitution.

The phrase "separation of church and state", does not appear in the Constitution. It has been traced to an 1802 letter written by Thomas Jefferson to the Danbury Baptists, where Jefferson spoke of the combined effect of the Establishment Clause and the Free Exercise Clause of the First Amendment. It has since been quoted in several legal opinions handed down by the United States Supreme Court.

The Separation of Church and State principle is a major aspect of our historical, legal, political, and social heritage. This principle preserves and protects our religious liberty. In the United States, the "Separation of Church and State" is generally discussed as a political and legal principle derived from the First Amendment of the United States Constitution. It reads, "Congress shall make no law respecting an establishment of religion, or prohibiting the free exercise thereof; or abridging the freedom of speech, or of the press; or the right of the people peaceably to assemble, and to petition the government for a redress of grievances." Historically, this is broken down into 2 clauses. These two clauses are known as the establishment clause and the free exercise clause.

The establishment clause is best interpreted as to prohibit the establishment of a national religion by Congress, or let Congress set a preference of one religion over another. This clause also prohibits the support of a religious idea with no identifiable secular purpose. This clause prohibits Congress from aiding religion in any way, even if such aid is made without regard to denomination.

The Free Exercise Clause reads, "Congress shall make no law respecting an establishment of religion, or prohibiting the free exercise thereof...". Issues of free exercise are also implicated by the extent to which laws are permitted to impinge upon private religious practice. In the United States, state laws can prohibit practices such as bigamy, sex with minors, drug use, and animal sacrifice. This can even be prohibited if the citizens claim the practices are part of their religious belief system.

It is the job of the federal courts to closely scrutinize any state or local laws that restrict the bona fide exercise of religious practices guaranteed by the Constitution. The federal courts ensure that genuine and important religious rights are not restricted, and that any questionable practices are limited only to the extent necessary. The courts demand that laws restricting religious practices demonstrate a "compelling" state interest, such as protecting citizens from bodily harm.

In simple terms, the Constitution means to protect all the religions from the state. It is not meant to protect the state from the religions. This means that any individual is entitled to express his faith in any religion. It also allows the person to be free from persecution, as long as it doesn't violate any laws. The Constitution also prohibits the U.S. from establishing a national religion.

Pledge of Allegiance

When the Pledge of Allegiance was written, it was done to honor our flag and to be patriotic. According to dictionary.com the word pledge means, "a solemn promise". Allegiance is defined as, "the loyalty of a citizen to his or her government or of a subject to his or her sovereign." Simply put the Pledge of Allegiance is an oath that Unites States citizens take to announce to the world that they are making a solemn promise to the U.S. Government. Sounds simple enough, until God was added to the pledge.

In August of 1892, Francis Bellamy (1855 - 1931), a Baptist minister, wrote the original Pledge of Allegiance. Bellamy was the chairman for a committee of state superintendents of education in the National Education Association. Part of his job as the chairman was to prepare the program for the public schools' quadricentennial celebration for Columbus Day. He designed the public school program around a flag raising ceremony and a flag salute. He decided to name it the "Pledge of Allegiance". Under the leadership of the American Legion and the Daughters of the American Revolution, the words of the Pledge were changed. The words, "my Flag", were changed to "the Flag of the United States of America". His original pledge is shown below.

"I pledge allegiance to my Flag and to the Republic for which it stands, one nation, indivisible, with liberty and justice for all".

Prior to June 14, 1923, there were no established federal or state regulations governing the display of the American Flag. It was on this date that the National Flag Code was adopted by the National Flag Conference. This conference was attended by representatives of the Army and Navy, which had designed their own procedures. This conference was attended also by some 66 other national groups. The regulation that was adopted for displaying the flag was based on the Army and Navy procedures. This guidance was adopted by all organizations in attendance and is still in effect.

US Flag

The U.S. Supreme Court has in the past ruled that school boards could compel all students to recite the Pledge, as it is deemed to be Patriotic. Most Jehovah's Witness children refuse to acknowledge the flag, due to their religious beliefs. Jehovah Witness's believe that the only one to whom worship should be given, is to God himself. Jehovah Witness's will never "salute" the flag of any country. They respect the flag and the government for which it stands, and they will not deface the flag, or treat it with any contempt in any way. They view protests, including flag burning as rebellion against God himself. Their rationale for this is that God allows these governments to stand in their position as authorities to help serve the greater good.

During the 1950's America, fear of communism was rampant. The Knights of Columbus begged Congress and drummed up enough support that Congress decided to add the words, "under God", to the Pledge. At this time, our country was dealing with McCarthyism and the fear of a growing Communist Party. The Pledge was now considered both a patriotic oath and a public prayer.

The First Amendment Center and the American Journalism Review released the results of a poll that was done on August 1, 2003. The poll found that 68% of adults believe that teachers who include "one nation under God" in the Pledge of Allegiance are not violating the principle of separation of church and state. The poll also found that 73% of respondents said that the pledge, including the "under God" phrase is "primarily a statement related to the American political tradition."

The Pledge of Allegiance is recited, on average, by tens of millions of times each day, mostly by students in schools across America. Personally, it seems that the more society withdraws from these traditions, the worse society becomes. We remove God from our lives, then bitterly complain to him when he isn't at our disposal. In today's modern society, there is more crime, poverty, illness, murder, war, and overall hardship. Makes you wonder. The more we push God out of our lives, the more crime, poverty, illness, murder, war, and overall hardship takes place. The biblical quote below shows where I believe our society is headed.

> "The people were so sinful, they cherished their hostility towards God that they refused to retain God in their knowledge, and so God gave them what they wanted." - Romans 1:28

Timeline of the Pledge

August 1892 - Francis Bellamy wrote the Pledge of Allegiance.

1923 - The words, "my Flag", were changed to "the Flag of the United States of America" by the American Legion and the Daughters of the American Revolution.

June 14, 1923 - National Flag Code was adopted at the National Flag Conference.

1940 - U.S. Supreme Court ruled that school boards could compel all students to recite the Pledge, as it is Patriotic.

1954- Congress decided to add the words, "under God", to the Pledge.

June 30, 2002 - Newsweek poll found that 9 in 10 Americans think the phrase "Under God" belongs in the Pledge of Allegiance

June 26, 2002 - 9th U.S. Circuit Court of Appeals voted 2 to 1 to declare the Pledge unconstitutional because of the addition of the phrase "under God."

June 26, 2002 - U.S. Senate passed a resolution with a vote of 99-0 supporting the use of "under God" in the pledge.

June 27, 2002 - U.S. House of Representatives passed a resolution 416-3 opposing the ruling of the 9th U.S. Circuit Court of Appeals.

November 13, 2002 - President Bush signed a bill reaffirmed keeping "under God" in the pledge, and "In God We Trust" as the United States national motto.

2003 - U.S. Representative Todd Akin of Missouri sponsored a bill, which would allow only the Supreme Court to review a constitutional challenge of the pledge.

February 2003 - Harris Interactive poll found that ninety percent of Americans say they believe in God.

August 1, 2003 - A First Amendment Center and the American Journalism Review poll found that 68% of people feel that "one nation under God" in the Pledge of Allegiance do not violate the principle of separation of church and state.

Dec. 19, 2003 - U.S. Justice Department filed a brief asking the U.S. Supreme Court to overturn the 9th U.S. Circuit Court of Appeals ruling.

September 14, 2005 - California District Judge ruled that the Pledge of Allegiance's phrase "under God" violates the rights of schoolchildren.

In God We Trust

"In God We Trust", is the official national motto of the United States. It is also the official motto for the State of Florida. Nowhere in the Bible does the phrase "In God We Trust" appear. It is with these four simple words that we can sum up our religious views.

Originally, the motto "In God We Trust" was placed on United States coins because of the increased religious sentiment that existed during the Civil War. The Secretary of the Treasury, Salmon P. Chase received many appeals from devout persons throughout the country, urging the United States to recognize God on its monetary coins. According to Treasury Department records, it appears that the first such appeal came in a letter written to Secretary Chase by Reverend M. R. Watkinson, a Minister of the Gospel from Ridleyville, Pennsylvania.

The motto, "In God We Trust" has been in continuous use on the one-cent coin since 1909. It has been included on the ten-cent coin since 1916. It also has appeared on all gold coins and silver dollar coins, half-dollar coins, and quarter-dollar coins struck since July 1, 1908.

President Eisenhower

In 1955, President Dwight D. Eisenhower signed Public Law 140, which made it mandatory for all United States currency to display the motto, "In God We Trust". This law applies to both coin and paper monies. "In God We Trust" was first used on paper money in 1957, when it appeared on the one-dollar silver certificate, which entered circulation on October 1st of that year. Since then all paper, currency issued has included the motto, "In God We Trust".

On February 15, 2007, some George Washington dollar coins were mistakenly struck without the edge inscriptions, including "In God We

Trust." It is believed that roughly 50,000 of these coins entered circulation. This coin has rapidly become a collector's item, as well as a source for conspiracy theorists.

Across the country, there is a movement among Atheists and Separationists. The Atheists and Separationists have been taking a pen in hand and obliterating the "In God We Trust" motto from the national
currency.

The Atheists and Separationists are breaking the law. Just because you do not agree with something, doesn't give you the right to deface it. Here is the law regarding the defacement of money. The Bureau of Engraving and Printing explains this violation. "Defacement of currency is a violation of Title 18, Section 333 of the United States Code. Under this provision, currency defacement is generally defined as follows: Whoever mutilates, cuts, disfigures, perforates, unites or cements together, or does any other thing to any bank bill, draft, note, or other evidence of debt issued by any national banking association, Federal Reserve Bank, or Federal Reserve System, with intent to render such item(s) unfit to be reissued, shall be fined not more than $100 or imprisoned not more than six months, or both." That would be like me living next door to Madalyn O'Hair and not liking the color of her home. I would have no right to change it. She has no right to change the appearance of money.

One of the first legal actions to challenge religious sloganeering of this type was made in 1978 by American Atheists founder Madalyn Murray O'Hair. The United States Supreme Court stated, "Its use is of a patriotic or ceremonial character and bears no true resemblance to a governmental sponsorship of religious exercise." The U.S. Court of Appeals for the Ninth Circuit also reached a similar conclusion.

Timeline of "In God We Trust"

It is easier to list the key dates of importance with regard to the allowing of the motto, "In God We Trust" to be placed on United States currencies. This motto sparks more controversy than any other area involving the "Separation of Church and State" debate. Listed below are the dates that I feel are most important to review.

November 13, 1861 - Reverend M. R. Watkinson appealed to the United States government to recognize God on its monetary coins.

April 22, 1864 - Congress passed the Act to include IN GOD WE TRUST on its coin currency.

March 3, 1865 - Act of Congress allowed the Mint Director, with the Secretary's approval, to place the motto "In God We Trust" on all gold and silver coins.

July 11, 1955 - President Dwight D. Eisenhower signed Public Law 140. This law made it mandatory that all U.S. coinage and paper currency to display the motto "In God We Trust."

July 30, 1956 - President Eisenhower approved Public Law 851. This was a Joint Resolution of the 84th Congress, declaring IN GOD WE TRUST the national motto of the United States.

October 1, 1957 - The first paper currency bearing the motto, In God We Trust entered circulation.

1978 - American Atheists challenged the religious sloganeering of "In God We Trust" as violating the separation of Church and State clause of the United States Constitution.

March 7, 2007 - U.S Mint reported some new George Washington dollar coins were mistakenly struck without the edge inscriptions, including "In God We Trust." This coin has rapidly become a collector's item, as well as a source for conspiracy theorists.

    I firmly believe that printing "In God We Trust" on our money is not stating our law. It is simply stating the belief of the majority of our countrymen. This is a belief that our ethics and morals are based on those of Him that created us.

The Ten Commandments

According to The Old Testament of the Bible, The Ten Commandments are one of the first gifts God gave to the nation of Israel when he freed them from slavery and brought them out of the land of Egypt.

Before I can even discuss the ten commandments, I must list them. The Ten Commandments are the ten primary laws God gave humans to follow and obey. The Ten Commandments are the moral statutes given by God, through Moses so that the Israelites could enjoy more fruitful and holy lives. The Ten Commandments are first mentioned in the book of Exodus.

> "And he was there with the LORD forty days and forty nights; he did neither eat bread, nor drink water. And he wrote upon the tables the words of the covenant, the ten commandments."
> - Exo 34:28

The Ten Commandments back then were also known as the "Law". In ancient Israel, breaking the Law was a serious offense. To deviate by any degree from the Ten Commandments was to sin and fall short of God's standard of holiness. The Ten Commandments reflect God's standard of holiness for everyone. God is considered to be the universal authority on moral conduct, and as such, all humans are subject to His standards.

According to the Bible, no one is exempt from God's Law. The ten commandments are listed below.

One - You shall have no other gods before Me.

Two - You shall not make for yourself a carved image--any likeness of anything that is in heaven above, or that is in the earth beneath, or that is in the water under the earth.

Three - You shall not take the name of the LORD your God in vain.

Four - Remember the Sabbath day, to keep it holy.

Five - Honor your father and your mother.

Six - You shall not murder.

Seven - You shall not commit adultery.

Eight - You shall not steal.

Nine - You shall not bear false witness against your neighbor.

Ten - You shall not covet your neighbor's house; you shall not covet your neighbor's wife, nor his male servant, nor his female servant, nor his ox, nor his donkey, nor anything that is your neighbor's.

    The Ten Commandments are very simple rules. If more people read them, understood them, and followed them there would be less problems in society. Many people today feel that God's Ten Commandments are no longer valid because they do not apply to our current and modernized society. These same people look to the Ten Commandments as being outdated and full of inflammatory language, which doesn't sit well with society's politically correct viewpoint. I guess these people feel it is okay to steal, kill, commit adultery, dishonor your parents, and lie. No wonder things are getting worse in the world.

Ten Commandments

"That thou mightest fear the LORD thy God, to keep all his statutes and his commandments, which I command thee, thou, and thy son, and thy son's son, all the days of thy life; and that thy days may be prolonged." - Deu 6:2

There is an ongoing dispute in the United States concerning the posting of the Ten Commandments on public property. People oppose the posting of the Ten Commandments on public property, arguing that it violates the establishment clause of the First Amendment to the Constitution of the United States. Other groups of people support the public display of the Ten Commandments. They claim that the displaying of the Ten Commandments is not necessarily a religious one, but a representation of the moral and legal foundation of society. They also feel that the Ten Commandments are appropriate to be displayed as a historical source of our present day legal codes.

On January 23, 1996, Minister Joe Wright was asked to open a session of the Kansas Senate. This prayer was given by Minister Joe Wright.

Reverend Wright

"Heavenly Father, we come before you today to ask your forgiveness and to seek your direction and guidance. We know Your Word says, 'Woe to those who call evil good,' but that is exactly what we have done. We have lost our spiritual equilibrium and reversed our values. We have exploited the poor and called it the lottery. We have rewarded laziness and called it welfare. We have killed our unborn and called it choice. We have shot abortionists and called it justifiable. We have neglected to discipline our children and called it building self-esteem. We have abused power and called it politics. We have coveted our neighbor's possessions and called it ambition. We have polluted the air with profanity and pornography and called it freedom of expression. We have ridiculed the time-honored values of our forefathers and called it enlightenment. Search us, Oh, God, and know our hearts today; cleanse us from every sin and set us free. Amen!"

Truer words were never spoken.

God's Ten Commandments are still the standard by which we should strive to live our lives. They are not some outdated laws that were only to be used by Moses. God intended that the Ten Commandments be mankind's permanent guidelines that we are still to follow in order to have a more meaningful relationship with God and each other.

> "Now these are the commandments, the statutes, and the judgments, which the LORD your God commanded to teach you, that ye might do them in the land whither ye go to possess it:" - Deu 6:1

School Prayer

There is **NO** aspect of the separation of church and state controversy that arouses more emotion and discussion, than the subject of allowing prayer in the public schools. Public schools are supported with taxpayer money. What taxpayer who believes in God would want their taxes to support an institution that prohibits their children from praying? On the other side, what atheist would want their taxes to support an institution that requires their children to participate in prayer?

What should be considered school prayer? Is it the student saying grace before a meal? Could it be the group of students studying the bible together? Do you consider it school prayer for the football coach to ask God to keep his players safe and free from injury? Simply defined, school prayer in its most common usage refers to the state sanctioned prayer by students in state schools.

President Clinton

President Bill Clinton on May 30, 1998 said, "Schools do more than train children's minds. They also help to nurture their souls by reinforcing the values they learn at home and in their communities.

I believe that one of the best ways we can help out schools to do this is by supporting students' rights to voluntarily practice their religious beliefs, including prayer in schools.... For more than 200 years, the First Amendment has protected our religious freedom and allowed many faiths to flourish in our homes, in our work places and in our schools. Clearly understood and sensibly applied, it works."

In today's era of violence and chaos, there is not a single institution in society where children are taught the values of life, as the community would like promoted. The government is too busy with geopolitical issues and the church is not allowed to inter. If children were taught in school the responsibilities of a code of conduct according to God, and how to apply this code as a guide to individual and group behavior there would be fewer problems. Children should be educated to participate in lawful, rational and constructive activities, while shunning whatever is evil, corrupting, addictive, or injurious.

School

On June 25, 1962, the United States Supreme Court heard and found that it is unconstitutional for state officials to compose an official school prayer and require its recitation in public schools. The court decided that government directed prayer in public schools is an unconstitutional violation of the Establishment Clause. The court's decision was decided by a vote of 6-1. This judgment became the basis for several subsequent decisions limiting government directed prayer in school.

In 1985, the Supreme Court ruled Alabama's law permitting one minute for prayer or meditation in school was unconstitutional. Also, the court in 1992 prohibited clergy led prayer at high school graduation ceremonies.

In 2002, the Court extended the ban to school sanctioning of student led prayer at high school football games.

> "And all things, whatsoever ye shall ask in prayer, believing, ye shall receive." - Mat 21:22

Anti prayer, proponents believe that public schools exist to educate, not to proselytize. Children in public schools are a captive audience. Anti prayer, proponents truly believe making prayer an official part of the school day is coercive and invasive. To introduce religion in our public schools builds walls between children who may not have been aware of any religious differences.

As a Registered Nurse, I find it amazing how many so proclaimed Atheists beg for a minister to help them talk to God as they are dying. They want to ask for God's help to end their suffering, help their families, and for forgiveness. It is a shame that a whole life is spent denying God until the end.

Faith Based Initiative

President Bush's Faith-Based Initiative originated from the simple idea that society's best chance to overcome a community's deepest problems is to tackle them by welcoming those community partners who truly know how to affect change in their community. When I first heard that President George Bush created the White House Office of Faith-based and Community Initiatives (CFBCI) I was shocked. Sounds way too close to the separation of church and state issue.

So what the heck is CFBCI? The initiative seeks to strengthen the faith based community organizations and expand their capacity. This is done through federally funded social services, with the idea being that these groups are well situated to meet the needs of local individuals. Simply put, CFBCI empowers faith based and community organizations to compete more effectively for Federal funds so that they may provide better human services to more people.

President Bush

"The paramount goal is compassionate results, and private and charitable groups, including religious ones, should have the fullest opportunity permitted by law to compete on a level playing field..." - President George W. Bush.

Critics of the CFBCI, include the Americans United for Separation of Church and State and the American Civil Liberties Union. They assert that it violates the Establishment Clause by using tax money to fund religion. It does make you kind of wonder. For the year 2005, more than $2.2 billion in competitive social service grants was awarded to faith-based organizations.

Faith based organizations are also eligible to participate in federally administered social service programs to the same degree as any other group. There are however certain restrictions. These restrictions have been created by the White House to protect the separation of church and state. The organizations may not use direct government funds to support inherently religious activities such as prayer, worship, or religious instruction. Any inherently religious activities that the organizations may offer must be offered separately in at a time or location from services that receive federal assistance. Finally, the organizations cannot discriminate on the basis of religion when providing their services.

The main focus of the President's initiative is to identify and eliminate barriers that impede the full participation in the Federal grants process. The program is also supposed to ensure that Federally funded social services administered by State and local governments are consistent with equal treatment provisions.

The initiative hopes to encourage a greater corporate and philanthropic support for the faith-based programs. The final focus is to pursue legislative efforts that would extend charitable choice provisions that prevent discrimination against faith-based organizations. Also, its purpose is to use legislation to help protect the religious freedom of beneficiaries, and preserve the religious hiring rights of faith-based charities.

Evolution Versus Genesis

Either God created the Garden of Eden with Adam and Eve or there are monkeys in our family tree. Two theories abound about man's beginnings. They are Genesis and Evolution. Proponents of life through the blessing of God believe that mankind was created and put here on the earth by an intelligent and Almighty Creator for a definite purpose? Who knows what is that purpose? Also, why is humanity so totally unaware of it?

On the other hand, the evolutionists believe and wonder, "Did human life develop over a period of millions of years from lower animal species by the process of evolution? Did humans as Darwin believed come to be formed and shaped as we are purely by natural causes and resident forces?" These are the two possibilities of our origin.

Listed below is the Biblical version of the Seven Days of Creation. All are excerpts from Genesis in the bible.

    Day One - Light
    Day Two - Sky and Waters
    Day Three - Plants
    Day Four - Sun, Moon, and Stars
    Day Five - Sea and Flying Creatures
    Day Six - Land Animals and Man
    Day Seven - Rest

On the first day, God created the light. "In the beginning, God created the heavens and the earth.

The earth was without form and void, and darkness was over the face of the deep. ... And God said, "Let there be light," and there was light. ... And God separated the light from the darkness. God called the light Day, and the darkness he called Night. And there was evening and there was morning, the first day." (Gen. 1:1-5)

On the second day, God made the Sky and Waters. God said, "Let there be an expanse in the midst of the waters, and let it separate the waters from the waters." And God made the expanse and separated the waters..." And it was so. (Gen. 1:6-8)

On the third day, God grew the Plants. God said, "Let the earth sprout vegetation, plants yielding seed, and fruit trees bearing fruit in which is their seed, each according to its kind, on the earth." ... And the earth brought forth vegetation... plants... and trees. (Gen. 1:9-13)

On day, four of creation God created the Sun, Moon, and Stars. Then God said, "Let there be lights in the expanse of the heavens to separate the day from the night, and let them be for signs and for seasons and for days and years, and let them be for lights in the expanse of the heavens to give light on the earth,"' and it was so. God made the two great lights, the greater light to govern the day, and the lesser light to govern the night; He made the stars also. (Gen. 1:14-19)

God on day five brought forth all the Sea and Flying Creatures. He said, "Let the waters swarm with swarms of living creatures, and let the birds fly above the earth"... so God created the great sea creatures and every living creature that moves with which the waters swarm... according to their kinds, and every winged bird according to its kind. (Gen. 1:20-23)

On the sixth day, God made the Land Animals and Man. God said, "Let the land produce living creatures according to their kinds: livestock, creatures that move along the ground, and wild animals, each according to its kind." And it was so... Then God said, "Let us make man in our image, after our likeness... So God created man in his own image. (Gen. 1:24-31)

Finally, God rested on the Seventh day. "Thus the heavens and the earth were finished, and all the host of them. And on the seventh day, God ... rested ... from all his work that he had done. So God blessed the seventh day and made it holy." (Gen. 2:1-3)

The problem for religious belief proponents is that science has explained a lot of odds and ends about the world. There is a second source of tension. These explanations have cast increasing doubt on the special role of man, as an being created by God.

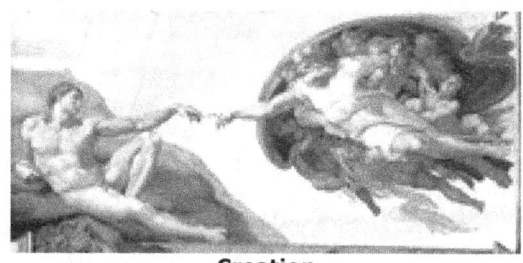

Creation

Science may be able to explain our creation, but the Bible lays it all out perfectly. The creation of the world is one of the most common Bible stories told. In six days, God created the entire universe. It is the first moment of the world's history, and it shows the awesome might and power of God. Many Christians interpret the story differently. Some take it literally. God simply created everything in six twenty four hour days. Other people, myself included have a variety of theories. My theory is that God created the world over a space of six ages and not days. To mankind a day is 24 hours. No one knows how much time is truly in a day for God. I believe that the days the Bible mentions are not literal days, but actually periods of time.

The most important discovery for the anti-creation proponents so far has been by Charles Darwin and Alfred Russel Wallace. Their theory of evolution shows that humans arose from earlier animals through natural selection acting on random heritable variations. They also believed that there was no need for a divine plan to explain the advent of humanity. This discovery led some, including Darwin, to lose their faith. Darwin as a young man had studied to be a Minister.

This discovery has been a source of tension between science and religion. Traditional religions generally rely on authority. This authority is an infallible leader, such as a prophet or a pope or a body of sacred writings, like the Bible or Koran. The big problem with the Darwin's theory of evolution is that it cannot explain where it all began.

"For what if some did not believe? Shall their unbelief make the faith of God without effect?"
- Rom 3:3

The theory of evolution has become widely accepted and caused the Bible to be viewed with hostility. Makes me wonder what has changed? A few centuries ago, laws prevented the teaching of the theory of evolution. The Bible was commonly accepted as the true and reliable account of our origins. Now almost the opposite is true. The Bible is banned from classrooms in American schools, and serious discussion of the biblical view of the creation of our universe and our human origins is forbidden. Meanwhile criticism of the theory of evolution is at times ruthlessly suppressed in academic and scientific circles. Why, I wonder would people try to avoid criticizing the theory of evolution? Makes me wonder who has to gain from this suppression? The answer is obvious. Scientists gain at the expense of society. If God is real, then there is not much need for science.

Scientists believe that the universe all started with a bang. This theory has come to be known as the "Big Bang Theory". This cosmological theory believes that the universe originated approximately 20 billion years ago from the violent explosion of a very small agglomeration of extremely high density and high temperature matter.

The Big Bang is a scientific theory. As a theory, it stands or falls by its agreement with observations. As a theory, which addresses, or at least seems to address, the origins of reality, it has always been entangled with theological and philosophical implications. In the 1920s and '30s, almost every major cosmologist preferred an eternal universe, and several complained that the beginning of time implied by the Big Bang imported religious concepts into physics. Sounds to me like Day One for Gods Creation of Man.

Picture of Universe

In 1972, the California State Board of Education asked NASA director Wernher von Braun, who is known as the father of the American space program, for his thoughts on the origin of the universe, life and the human race. This is his statement, "To be forced to believe only one conclusion—that everything in the universe happened by chance—would violate the very objectivity of science itself. Certainly, there are those who argue that the universe evolved out of a random process, but what random process could produce the brain of a man or the system of the human eye? They challenge science to prove the existence of God. But must we really light a candle to see the sun?."

I ask, If human beings are the top of the evolutionary process, how is it that we have the disadvantage of requiring a member of the opposite sex to reproduce? Lower forms of life such as bacteria, viruses and protozoa are sexless and far more prolific? If they can reproduce by far simpler methods, why can't we? If evolution is an absolute truth, what went wrong? Darwin and mankind have overlooked such obvious flaws in the theory of evolution. It is easier for mankind to deny God and not be held accountable for our transgressions.

Here is a few words to live by for all of mankind, no matter your religious beliefs. Man should learn from the past, plan for our future, and enjoy the present, while tempering our behavior with prudence and consideration for others.

> "And the great dragon was cast out, that old serpent, called the Devil, and Satan, which deceiveth the whole world: he was cast out into the earth, and his angels were cast out with him." - Rev 12:9

Are We Better With or Without God?

Are religious societies better than secular ones? Do they have less divorce, murder, theft, and problems? It should be an easy question for atheists to answer. Many of those now seeking to blow people up whether with tanks and missiles, or rucksacks and passenger planes do so in the name of God. The most dangerous human trait is an absence of self-doubt. Self-doubt is more likely to be absent from the mind of the believer than the infidel. Few religious governments have committed atrocities on the scale of Hitler's, Mao's or Stalin's. I will examine whether life is better with or without God. The decision is yours to make.

History tells us that God punished the House of Israel through the hand of their enemy, the Assyrian nation. The people of the northern kingdom of Israel were either killed or deported into slavery.

> "Moreover I also gave them My Sabbaths, TO BE A SIGN between them and Me that they might know that I am the LORD who sanctifies them. Yet the House of Israel rebelled against Me in the wilderness; they did not walk in My statutes; they despised My judgments, which if a man does, he shall live by them; and they greatly DEFILED MY SABBATHS. Then I said I would pour out My fury on them." - Ezekiel 20:12-13

Religion is important in this country. Even with the separation of church and state, no one who expressed doubt about the existence of God could possibly be elected or has been elected President of the United States. Many Americans fervently believe that religion is a good thing, and get quite angry when it is criticized.

In all religions, God allocates rewards and punishments according to our actions and thoughts, either in this life or the next. The concept of divine judgment is not based on any observed property of the cosmos, nor on any objective evidence. Forgiveness is a necessary component of a judging God if he is to enforce norms and religious beliefs. Many people believe that the wrath of God is a human invention. This wrath is designed to reinforce norms of social behavior. If you believe in a one true God and his Ten Commandments, you know it is a divine intervention, not a human invention. Religious beliefs, backing them with the threat of God and legal system offer greater reach and efficiency than any human one. If all of mankind had a bit of the fear of God, it would be a better world.

> "Go and cry unto the gods which ye have chosen; let them deliver you in the time of your tribulation." - Jdg 10:14

Man has to embrace two fundamental guidelines. The first is that there exists an all-powerful, all knowing and most wise God who has endowed man with the natural ability for righteous living. The second guideline is that our sincere efforts to live righteously always please God and usually contribute to our common welfare and personal well-being.

Church Etiquette

What is etiquette? Etiquette is simply "rules of acceptable behavior". I bet you remember the time when people put on their "Sunday best" to go to church. In fact, our best clothes are often referred to as our "Sunday clothes". A church service is an offer of devotion and as a matter of respect, it is therefore appropriate to wear one's best attire.

In our modernized and relaxed society, dress in church has become too casual. Think about it. You are going to worship your creator and savior. We dress up to go out on a date, but go to Church in casual clothes. We should be offering Christ our best, and not our everyday or common wear. We should dress modestly, not in a flashy way that would bring attention to ourselves. Our dress should always be becoming of a Christian, especially at church.

Here are some specific guidelines from various sources. I am going to call these the **"Rule of Three"**.

Rule One: No one should wear T-shirts with any kind of writing on them.

Rule Two: Shorts, ripped clothes, or mini skirts are not appropriate church wear.

Rule Three: Only women should wear a hat in church.

Much of church etiquette is based on common sense and showing respect for God and others. Always remember that you are in church to worship God, the Holy Trinity. Christians Services reflect on respect, awe and appreciation of the Lord. The Rule of Three applies to adults and need not be seen for people with special needs or little children.

Upon entering the Church, speaking should quickly "de-escalate". Simply put, lower your voice. You are in the house of God and should show respect. Parishioners should not have any food or be chewing gum. Whenever the celebrant is reading aloud any of the prayers no unnecessary side conversations.

All of these things teach us respect for the Lord, teaching our souls and deepening our awareness of His presence, not only in Church but around us in everyday circumstances.

> "Wherefore now let the fear of the LORD be upon you; take heed and do it: for there is no iniquity with the LORD our God, nor respect of persons, nor taking of gifts". - 2Ch 19:7

Breakdown of Worldwide Religions

Religion sizes shown are only approximate estimates. There are many more religions in the world, but I picked the most popular and well known for this list.

1. Christianity: 2.1 billion
2. Islam: 1.5 billion
3. Secular/Agnostic/Atheist: 1.1 billion
4. Hinduism: 900 million
5. Chinese traditional religion: 394 million
6. Buddhism: 376 million
7. Primal-indigenous: 300 million
8. African Traditional & Diasporic: 100 million
9. Sikhism: 23 million
10. Juche: 19 million
11. Spiritism: 15 million
12. Judaism: 14 million
13. Baha'i: 7 million
14. Jainism: 4.2 million
15. Shinto: 4 million
16. Cao Dai: 4 million
17. Zoroastrianism: 2.6 million
18. Tenrikyo: 2 million
19. Neo-Paganism: 1 million
20. Unitarian-Universalism: 800 thousand
21. Rastafarianism: 600 thousand
22. Scientology: 500 thousand

Most religions have a common need, which is to <u>KNOW GOD</u>. All Christians believe that Jesus Christ is the Savior and the son of God. Even people of the Jewish faith believe Jesus Christ existed. They believe that he was a great teacher and example, but not the son of God. Satanists worship Satan, but even they believe in God. They have to believe in God, because they worship his opposite.

One of the hallmarks of any religion is their belief in a supernatural being or beings. They can take a variety forms, not all of which are found in every religion. The most common beliefs usually fall into one of five categories: animatisms, animism, ancestral spirits, gods or goddesses, and minor supernatural beings.

> "Beware of false prophets, which come to you in sheep's clothing, but inwardly they are ravening wolves." - Mat 7:15

Conclusion

Throughout my research, I have noticed that religious motto's are used in support of the notion that America is founded upon Christian religious principles. Did you know that the opening of congressional sessions begins with prayer? The US Supreme Court building displays a replica of the Ten Commandments. The President of the United States takes the oath of office while swearing on a bible. This same sort of evidence, though, often appears in court rulings, which decide establishment clause cases. Justices will often cite the "In God We Trust" motto.

> "Then hear thou in heaven their prayer and their supplication, and maintain their cause." - 1 Ki 8:45

Most Christians believe that God is trying to save the world. This thinking believes that God and the devil are in a constant state of war over the fate of mankind. This is seen as the desperate struggle between good and evil.

Never has the world had so much, yet been so miserable. More does not always mean for the better. We have satellite television, cellular phones, cars that cost more than homes. We have family and friends, many who we ignore. How much is enough? Ask yourself, where have we forgotten God? Sure, you go to church. That includes God for one hour out of 168 hours per week. Are you the type of Christian that offer thanks for all you have or do you only speak with God in a crisis? Mankind needs to perform some internal self-examinations.

A friend once asked me if I believe in God. I have no particular spiritual insight. I think that this world is just more than our simple existence. To me there is more to God, than just this universe. I definitely believe in a power greater than myself. When I die and if it turns out that I am wrong, I will never know. Imagine that you go through life saying there is no God and when you die, you are wrong. I would rather believe and have faith and have no after life, instead of denying God to find out he exists.

This poem was written and recited before Congress by Darrel Scott, a parent who lost his child during a senseless rampage at the American High School, know as Columbine. This senseless act shocked our nation to its core. In a way, this poem sums up the meaning behind this book.

> Your laws ignore our deepest needs,
> Your words are empty air.
> You've stripped away our heritage,
> You've outlawed simple prayer.
> Now gunshots fill our classrooms,
> And precious children die.
> You seek for answers everywhere,
> And ask the question "Why?"
> You regulate restrictive laws,
> Through legislative creed.
> And yet you fail to understand,
> That God is what we need!

God Bless and Keep the Faith!

Religious Web Sites

Belief Net
www.beliefnet.com

Bible.com Ministries
www.bible.com

Bible Study
www.biblestudy.org

Catholic Church
www.catholic.org

Church of God
www.churchofgod.org

Church of Latter Day Saints
www.mormon.org

Islam
www.islamworld.net

Jehovah's Witness
www.watchtower.org

Judaism
www.aish.com

Religious Tolerance
www.religioustolerance.org

Sikhism
www.sikhism.com

The Church of Wicca
www.wicca.org

The Hindu Universe
www.hindunet.org

United Methodist Church
www.umc.org

Worldwide Buddhist
www.buddhanet.net

Glossary

Agnostic - a person who holds that the existence of the ultimate cause, as God, and the essential nature of things are unknown and unknowable, or that human knowledge is limited to experience.

Ancestral spirits - belief system of most cultures consists of the souls or ghosts of ancestors.

Animatisms - A belief that all animate and inanimate objects are infused with a common life force.

Animism - belief in the existence of individual spirits that inhabit natural objects and phenomena.

Atheist - a person who denies or disbelieves the existence of a supreme being or beings.

Bible - the sacred writings of the Christian religion.

Bigamy - the practice of multiple marriage.

Bill of Rights - a formal statement of the fundamental rights of the people of the United States, incorporated in the Constitution as Amendments

Bishop - a person who supervises a number of local churches or a diocese, being in the Greek, Roman Catholic, Anglican, and other churches a member of the highest order of the ministry.

Buddhist - originated in India by Buddha, believing that life is full of suffering caused by desire and that the way to end this suffering is through enlightenment that enables one to halt the endless sequence of births and deaths to which one is otherwise subject.

Catholic - churches that have claimed to be representatives of the ancient undivided church.

Christian - a person who believes in Jesus Christ; adherent of Christianity.

Communist - a socioeconomic structure that promotes the establishment of an egalitarian, classless society based on common ownership of the means of production and property in general.

Constitution - the system of fundamental principles according to which a nation, state, corporation, or the like, is governed.

God - the one Supreme Being, the creator and ruler of the universe.

Goddess - female being of supernatural powers or attributes, believed in and worshiped by a people.

Gospel - the story of Christ's life and teachings, esp. as contained in the first four books of the New Testament, namely Matthew, Mark, Luke, and John.

Hitler - an Austrian-born politician who led the National Socialist German Workers Party, the Nazi Party.

Jehovah's Witness - a Christian group originating in the United States at the end of the 19th century by

Charles Taze Russell, whose doctrine centers on the Second Coming of Christ.

Jesus Christ - Jesus of Nazareth. born 4 b.c., crucified a.d. 29. The source of Christian religion.

Jew - one of a scattered group of people that traces its descent from the Biblical Hebrews or Israelite.

Knights of Columbus - the world's largest Catholic fraternal service organization.

Mao - a Chinese military and political leader who led the Communist Party of China.

Martyr - a person who willingly suffers death rather than renounce his or her religion.

McCarthyism - term describing the intense anti-communist suspicion in the United States in a period, that lasted roughly from the late 1940s to the late 1950s.

Moses - a Biblical Hebrew religious leader, lawgiver, prophet, and military leader, to whom the authorship of the Torah is traditionally attributed.

Muslim - A believer in or adherent of Islam.

Paine, Thomas - an English pamphleteer, revolutionary, radical, inventor, and intellectual.

Pagan - a person or community observing a polytheistic religion, a person who is not a Christian, Jew, or Muslim.

Pope - the bishop of Rome as head of the Roman Catholic Church.

Protestant - any Christian group, which developed from the Reformation.

Romans - relating to ancient or modern Rome or its people or culture; or relating to the Roman Empire; A native, inhabitant, or citizen of ancient or modern Rome.

Saint - a person of great holiness, virtue, or benevolence.

Satan - profoundly evil adversary of God and humanity, often identified with the leader of the fallen angels; the Devil.

Stalin - party leader and dictator of the Soviet Union, established the regime now known as Stalinism.

Supernatural - relating to the immediate exercise of divine power; miraculous.

Wicca - a neo-pagan religion based on the pre-Christian traditions of England, Ireland, Scotland, and Wales. Its origins can be traced even further back to Paleolithic peoples who worshipped a Hunter God and a Fertility Goddess.

References

Bible.com Ministries
P.O. Box 850
Dewey, AZ 86327
www.bible.com

Brainy Quote
www.brainyquote.com

Britannica Encyclopedia
331 North La Salle Street
Chicago, IL 60610
www.Britannica.com

Department of the Treasury
1500 Pennsylvania Avenue, NW
Washington, D.C. 20220
www.ustreas.gov

Dictionary.com

Encyclopedia.com

Imageen Vision
541-245-8566
www.imageenvision.com

Thesaurus.com

Washington Post
P.O. Box 17370
Arlington, VA 22216
www.washingtonpost.com

White House
Office of Faith-Based and Community Initiatives
Washington, D.C. 20502
www.fbci.gov

Wikipedia Encyclopedia
200 2nd Ave. South #358
St. Petersburg, FL 33701-4313
www.wikipedia.org

About the Author

The Author has led an interesting life. He has worked in a variety of fields ranging from Restaurant Management, Licensed Seaman, Educator, Journalist, and, is currently a Registered Nurse working in a Community Hospital nestled in the Adirondack Mountains. Academically he has earned a variety of degrees, which are listed in chronological order: AA in Mass Media, BA in Communication Arts, AS in Nursing, and finally a MS in Health Care Administration. He lives with his wife, Virginia, and their two sons, John and Seamus in the Adirondack Mountains in upstate New York.

GOD 88

www.ingramcontent.com/pod-product-compliance
Lightning Source LLC
Chambersburg PA
CBHW032150040426
42449CB00005B/462